Confessions of a Teenage Poet

Bethany Ray Daigle

With love, always
write and be spontaneous!
Bethany Ray Daigle

Inspiration is the greatest thing in the world, especially when it comes from peers.

For my mom
and Agne Kelley

Scenery

"The poetry of the earth is
never dead."
- John Keats

Squirrel

Lil' squirrel hides in a wood.
Safe from harm of
The snow-covered lawn.
As darkness draws near,
It hears the owl,
Everywhere.
It slides its eyes closed,
And imagines.
That **it** was the big, powerful owl.
That **it** could find a home
And a mate by spring.
He nestles in his burrow
Of twigs and leaves,
Constantly aware—thinking.
He falls asleep to the owl's harsh cry
And wakes to the chickadee's bright song.
He made it through the night.

December 16, 2009

Winter

I sit inside looking outside and marveling at the
wonderful scenery.
I see many lawns evenly coated with snow,
They look simply like a sea of white.
My eyes travel, gaping at nearly everything in
sight,
Trees so covered with the simple pristine
That they seem as if they are staggering
mountaintops of pure white.
Ivory.
Everything seems to have been swept
In nothing but marvelous white, gray, and
silver.
The sun is out, making everything light
Shine and illuminate the trees incredibly.
I want so badly to go outside and
Make those first impressions
In that wonderfully frosted natural creation,
But.
It's below zero out there,
So I'll just watch.
I see delightful blue jays glide from
Aerie up high to aerie down low.
Deer scavenge underneath woods in search of

Corn and twigs that haven't been found,
For their supper.
Winter, my favorite season.
Too bad only a portion of the world
Has the opportunity to view this absolute
Elegance.
Some disdainful people take one glance at the
New,

fluffy snow,
Moan and then walk off.
Other optimistic people, however,
Smile at every snowfall.

February 1, 2010

Outside

A wilderness so stunningly serene,
It causes city slickers within close-quarters
To marvel at the hue its beauty creates.
A stream runs wild with
Freshwater trout from Lake Superior.

Birds sing a bright tale,
Notifying everyone around that winter

Is finally over.

Redwood trees tower over everything—
As far as the eye can see.
New buds on apple trees bloom to the
Steady beat of life and wonder.

Deer run free through a meadow,
Filled with daises and wildflowers so divine,
As rabbits go to meet
Their families across the clearing once again.

At this joyous time,
All creatures that were exposed to the
The frigid, shivering, never-ending chill of
This year's miserable winter,
Now run outside of their burrows,
And embrace the warming sunlight of spring.

January 4, 2010

Up

The place I usually see:
a palace of clouds,
a castle of air crystals,

a place where the angels sing.
As I daydream about it,
it feels as it is just simply
a figment of my imagination.
But it is there—I know it.
For it is the place I have traveled
over a million times to and back.
I throw my head back while humming
a delightfully hearty tune of my childhood,
and I gaze at the exquisitely divine skies.
Up.
Where magic exists.
Up.
Where there is peace for everyone.
Up.
Where all hope to be going someday.

January 5, 2010

Rain

You are music to my ears.
I love the pitter-patter-drip-drop
Falling continually, never breaking stride,
Running as smooth as a marathon runner.

It makes me smile dumbly at how
All the birds stay away,
While I'm out splashing in your puddles,
Feeling very gleeful.

How you make the grass so green
Will never cease to amaze me.
Right now our lawn looks like
The Super Bowl turf,
All bright, with no dead spots.

I'm a city girl stuck in the country,
So I guess you could say I'm
Used to noticing endless streams of you,
Flowing gently off the road.

I'm truly inspired with you,
The way you appear, fall, and leave
So the sun returns in only minutes, usually,
Is a beautiful thing to ponder over.

I especially love it when you wake me
In the middle of the night,
A soft, sweet lullaby I am not aware of.
It just drips and drops, making the most
precious midnight music,
Floating in the background so simply,

Like how the highway is for city people.

You send a great smell to me.
It makes me think the ocean
Would smell like this;
A combination of newly mowed grass,
Fresh flowers,

And late-morning dew.
As soon as you stop falling from the heavens,
A robin chirps its thoughts.
I won't forget this time the sky showered on
me, for once.

April 30, 2010

Clouds

Whenever I am frustrated,
I look to you.
I become lost in the ever-changing creations
That float so sweetly through the sky.
Wait—what was that?
I swear it was a heart.
But it's gone now, something else.
I smile,
Remembering how once,

You were the only thing I could confide in;
Could talk about nothing in particular for
hours and hours,
Could receive life-changing advice from.
Those days are gone, though!
I'm doing well, thanks for asking.
Actually, I'm feelings about as high as you —
Careless,
Full of energy,
Wonderful,
Simply perfect.

May 16, 2010

Flower
A simple seed,
A small hole in the earth.
A few drops of water and
A little sunlight a day
Makes a beautiful creation.
A tulip, rose, or daffodil.
It really doesn't take much to
Generate the wonderful aroma making
Plant that brightens people's days.
I love walking out in an enclosure,
Submerged in the rainbows of

Colors, sweet smells, and soft textures.
I'm going to sift out a bundle of blossoms
To make a ravishing display
For my dining room table.
It smells like summer;
It should always smell the way
it does right now.
Happiness is exerted so much it's
Practically pouring out,
Spreading its influence to the world.

May 21, 2010

Fog

All you do is hang around me,
An unforgiving cloud of unpleasantness.
Won't singing some silly song,
Like for rain, make you go away?
No?
I thought so.
Well, don't you realize how much of a hazard
you are?
You make harmless old people and
Innocent fresh drivers crash.
You cause thousands of dollars in repairs.
You bring a smell that is a
Very unpleasant mixture of

Sea salt, dying sunflowers, and
When car exhaust is included in that combo,
It is downright dreadful.
I don't mean to sound cross,
But I would much rather see the
Beautiful, happy rays of sunshine
And birds flitting about,
Than your hideously plain complexion.

April 10, 2010

Friends

"The friendship that can cease
has never been real."
- St. Jerome

Cat

You once guarded me all night long,
As I slept.
But now as I play very happily,
You rest.

I have watched endlessly of you,
Batting your big, soft paws at an
Old, worn out, tattered shoelace.
I still recall how the sparkle of glee
Never left your eyes.

I remember very clearly of how
When I was sick with a cold or the flu,
You never left my bed.
It was almost as if you were
Determined to heal me with your purrs.

I smirk dumbly at the memory of you,
When you brought a dead mouse to my door.
You seemed so proud,
So exuberant that I loved your gift.

I sure wish I would have recorded
All those perfect times when you

Jumped and pranced and pounced around

In the backyard,
Hoping you would get lucky enough
To catch a butterfly, with your teeth.

I love that look of sheer contentment
You give me as I fall asleep.
The light caress of your tail,
When you would occasionally flick your tail.

The quiet serenade of your purrs,
Motor-boating around my consciousness until I
sleep.

Cat,
You are the best animal that
I have ever known.
I thank you so much for the impeccable
memories.

January 9, 2010

Baby

I cradle you in my arms,
Singing you a soft, happy lullaby.
I watch you furl and unfurl your fingers
Around my long, auburn hair.
I croon how your eyelashes flutter
With each yawn you make.
I love how you scrunch when you inhale
And the whistle you make
As you exhale.
I admire the way your cute red curls dangle
From your perfectly round head,
The size of the most beautiful orange in the
world.
You are just simply adorable.
You're my baby.
I love you!

January 12, 2011

Emmy

A creative sister.
A music lover of all types—
Except old-time rock and roll.
She devours books by the series.'

She's an incredible scenery printer,
That watches movies in her spare time.
She is also a very fun person to play the Wii
with.
Her shiatsu Charlie loves to play.
She always gives me good advice when I'm
confused,
And cheers me up when I'm down.
She makes me laugh about
Stupid, silly, dumb, hilarious old memories.
She talks to me about her life,
And listens to me when I tell her about my
dreams.
She is the best kind of sister for me.
I love her.

March 3, 2010

Dog

Loyal, Playful, Happy.
Always by my side.
Warns me of an intruder.
Makes me burst in laughter
When I think I might explode in tears.
He keeps me warm when laying by me.

He continually urges me to play a little more
with the ball
And always wants to walk around the block,
With his tiny leash in my hand, a bit more,
For he is such a demanding pooch.
Thanks dog,
For being my unconditional best friend.

April 7, 2010

Rocking Chair

It was there,
In that rocking chair,
That you read us stories before bedtime,
All of us scattered on the floor.

Where you would feed the baby
Her bottle and maybe
(On a good night)
would sing her to sleep.

Where you would sit
For hours at a time,
Concentrating so immensely on your
Knitting to sell on the shore.

Where you taught us about
Life and love and
Why we shouldn't shout.
Thanks, Grandma.
I love you!

November 2, 2011

Trampoline

Step back.
Big breath.
Immediate burst of speed.
Shooting right for the trampoline.
Slow down slightly.
Lean forward.
Grasp the rim.
Pull body over.
Lay down.
Close eyes.
Relax for a moment.
Open eyes and remember....
All the times we've made up games that
Involve us jumping as high as we can.
All the times we sat there looking at each other,

Trying to guess the songs on our minds.
All the times we made really goofy faces at
each other
And couldn't stop laughing.
All the times we played truth-or-dare
Till dusk, giving silly, dumb dares.
All the times we looked for hours
For the easiest constellations.
All the times we wanted to get away from
Your little brother, laughing recurrently.

All the times when you were trying to
Read me an article from a magazine
While everyone was bouncing up and down.
I'm thinking of going on
That trampoline once again,
To see if I will erupt in laughter like before.
I guess all that's left to see is:
"Man, that was fun!"

April 12, 2010

A Poem for Agne

With tearful eyes,
We caught glimpses of our own demise,
As she slowly began to fade away.

God realized Agne
Was growing more and more tired,
And a cure was not to be.

He bent down
Next to her with the smallest frown,
And whispered in her ear,
"come with me, you don't need to fear."

Not long after that happened,
She was gone, and we all immediately
grew saddened.

I never even got to say,
"Goodbye, best friend. I'll see you again
some day."

May 2010

Memory

There is nothing quite like a memory of a mom.
Because even if she has gone,
She continues to live;
In our heart and mind forever.
We shall be eternally blessed by the
Wonderful teachings and insights along the
way, throughout our lives.
So,
Even if she has gone,
It is required f us to replay scenes
Where she was very proud of us
And told us how much she loves us.
We must never forget that,
Because after all,
Moms are what make the whole world.

March 6, 2011

9/11

Today is September 11th,
The 10th anniversary of the Twin Towers'
bombing.
There, sadness and anger leaked across our
country,
Like a crazy river.
Millions of precious memories were
Covered with the soot brought by the
Dreadful Al Qaeda bomb.
We Americans have lost a dreadful amount on
that day.
But, through these past 10 years,
We've gained new technologies such as the
iPad,
Thousands of bright, baby births,
And how to deal with anger and regret to
become a better nation.
Though we will never create something to
measure up to
The loss of the Twin Towers,
We have created Ground Zero,
A tribute to all the innocent lives that had
perished 10 years ago.
No matter what happens, never think that

things couldn't be worse,
Because this impact on our nation,
Certainly shows they can.

September 11, 2011

Thoughts

"Keep your feet on the
ground, and your thoughts
at lofty heights."
- Peace Pilgrim

School

I feel trapped here,
For an eight-hour day,
Five times a week.
Having teachers cram as much
"Learning" as they can within a
Forty-five minute period
Is not fun at all for me.
Some kids gaze for a long while
At the pile of homework lingering on their
desk,
Completely astonished that one teacher
COULD
Assign that much work.
And hey, getting lectured whenever
something's
Done incorrectly isn't exactly a joy ride either.
Why must we wait until the bell rings,
To be dismissed to mingle in the hallways,
Before another class?
I grow very tired of sitting lethargically
Watching the younger kids run around at
recess,
When I'm shunned inside.
I saunter through the school,

Barely hearing the buzz of jocks and players
freak about
The game-winning basketball shot or
Preppy-girl gossip of who's with whom.
A blink…
And I'm out the door.
Falling into the endless stream of
Zombified kids wandering aimlessly about the
Hallway to their lockers with their friends.
This…
Is my life for the next four years.
Mom says I better enjoy it,
For it'll be the best time of my life.

January 21, 2010

Books

I might drown,
Deep in the invisible adventure awaiting me.
I may not return to the surface—
Edward could have taken my breath away.
I may b held forever in the never-ending story
With fantastic protagonists like
Percy Jackson, Zoey Redbird, Erik Night, Jacob
Black, Vladimir Tod, D'Ablo, Iggie, Salz,

Summer, Rosco, Bethany, Gabriel, Gretchen,
and every single one.
Their lives may not exist in out time,
And that is the reason in which we must
Jump past the barriers of
Reality into fiction, fantasy, romance, etcetera.
We all should make that daring, effortless,
simple jump at least once a day.
Read a good book!

February 11, 2010

Tired

I can barely keep my eyes open.
I yawn very frequently.
All I can manage to do successfully is toss and
turn
While watching George Lopez.
I get a glare from my cat, and she leaves.
Alright.
Television off.
I get comfortable.
Now for the wait.
The excruciating yet lovely wait for sleep,

sweet sleep.
I pry my eyes open once more
And search frantically for the clock in the dark.
The bright red digits flash 2:31.
Ohhh, boy.
This is going to be one very long night.
After I endured one more yawn,
I thrust my eyes shut again....

... ...

BEEP BEEP BEEP!
Before I knew it, my alarm was yelling at me to
wake up.
Sheesh, I get it already!
Well, at least I got SOME sleep.

February 22, 2010

Dress

I walk passed the window display and see you;
Your black velvet-looking sleeves,
Your very sleek dark blue skirt,
Your gorgeous, glittery belt at the waist,
Your elegant, ebony purple collar, and,

Who could forget your price tag?
So sleek, gorgeous, and chic.
But why do you have to cost so much?
I walk away from you and your beckoning
ways.
Though I know I'd regret it,
Someday.

April 8, 2010

I D U

I don't understand.
Why people think they're "cool"
When hurting those around them.

How people can be so mean,
Don't they ever feel guilty?

Why can't we just let things go,
Be like the wind and blow it away?

Could people ever learn to respect one another,
Instead of rejecting?

How can animals sense
Whenever I am upset?

Why must they fight,
It is not at all a pretty sight…
How people think I'm not a poet,
When secretly, they know they know it.

February 3, 2011

Library

People come in—people go out.
Making black scuff-marks on
The freshly cleaned yellow linoleum.

The door melodically chimes
Whenever someone arrives,
Or leaves.

That old scanner's continuous beep
As books are nonchalantly
Checked in and out.

There is always a thud from books;
Being carefully opened,

Callously closed,
Delicately put away,
And banged benign on the table.

Children burst;
Some in bright, bubbly laughter,
Some in deep, sorrow-filled sadness,
Some in antagonizing, irate anger.

At a desk nearby,
The librarian smacks her
Wrinkled, chapped, lips
And wags a finger while thinking of atrocities
At the book-loving kids.

December 17, 2009

If Heaven Were a Food

If Heaven were a food,
I would never get fat.
I could sit and eat as many
Twinkies and chocolate bars and potato
chips
As I dared to.
Heaven would be something
delightfully light and airy, like cotton

Candy.
But yet, it would hold its consistence,
Like brand new caramel.

Heaven would know when to make
A delicious food
Crack or break under pressure,
And if it had super powers.

If heaven were a food,
One bite could fill you up so you
Would be able to continue your long
adventure in the mountains,

Or it could take 10,000 bites for you to be
full,
Enabling you to eat much more of your
favorite food.

In heaven, there would be no such thing
as "Too much sweets."
I would be able to pig out and feast upon
Laffy Taffy and butterscotch and Sprees,
As much I would like!

If heaven were a food,
Some foods would suck your fat away,

Almost like a vacuum.
SHOOOM!
Your belly fat was just absorbed in a new
Belly Bar.

In Heaven,
It wouldn't be 'against the rules'
To marry a sandwich,
Or even have an abomination such as
"Breakfast only until noon."

In Heaven,
All foods could live in harmony.
A place where happy foods like
Lasagna and pancakes and Twinkies
Could make an acceptable meal.

If heaven were a food,
It would my favorite place in the whole
universe.
I would never, ever leave,
Because I love food.

January 23, 2014

My Sanctuary

As I turn the door knob
To my special place,
I brace myself for the
Color intensity I will soon see.

The doors open and
Immediately my previous
Thoughts are left behind me.
As I gape around, I see…

Posters covering two walls;
A dresser that can indeed be de-cluttered;
Green wicker chairs on either side of the
dresser.
An additional splash of color
On a lamp, behind a chair,
Each fitted with
Quilts that drape the backs of their comfiness;
Bright green curtains perfectly match
The equally vibrant green walls;
A trundle bed is equipped with
My sewing machine and proper accessories;
A book on a pillow;
A cat yawning;

There are multi-colored rugs
Strewn about all over the floor, exposing the
cold concrete;
There is a closet full of clothes and shoes;
And even another closet filled
With shelves stacked with books and
Cute, fun little things acquired throughout the
years.

This....
Is my wonderful sanctuary.
I exhale as reality
Is swept back over me,
Like a light, soothing, slap in the face.

I close the entrance to my room,
And walk away,
Lighter than air with
A sense of at-ease and nostalgia sweeping over
me.

January 9, 2010

Music

My melody.
My inspiration.
My peace-giver.
My connection to the human race.
My at-home relaxer.
My stress-reliever.
My time waster.
My sadness.
My anger.
My joy.
My music.
December 19, 2009

Bethany

"Nothing builds self-esteem
and self-confidence like
accomplishment."
- Thomas Carlyle

My Day

Feeling groggy and gross,
I hop in the shower and
Let go of all my filth.

I scrub my luscious locks,
Thinking it would be easier if
I just cut it all off.

I fall,
Just outside the shower stall.

I stumble down to my room,
Where I begin to groom.

A touch of eyeliner there,
I hope my mom doesn't care.

I find a really cute blouse
And decide to walk about the house.

I clutch my phone,
And magically, all of my messages are shown.

I stare openly at the fruit,
Then I take a bite from the loot.

I pet my dog,
Who acts like a hog.

I say hello to my cat,
And she snaps back.

I call my boyfriend,
Sad when the conversation ends.
I update my status,
And clean the lattes.

I draw a picture and
Notice the dust in the light fixture.

I do a bit of sewing
While the wind's a-blowing.

I play the Sims 2,
And who wouldda knew!
My Saturday just ended.
But until the last text is sended.

March 6, 2011

Bubbles

Some days I feel as if I am
Trapped inside a bubble.
No matter how hard I try,
I just can't break free.
No matter what I say,
No one truly listens anyway.
I get so frustrated with myself,
For being so quiet,
When what I really wanted to do
Was SCREAM and SHOUT.
I hate feeling this fragile,
Anything said about me
Being STUPID or a BITCH
Makes me simply,
Shutdown.
I try to escape the escalating tears,
And find myself
Out of exits.
How funny it is,
That I am talking about being
Cornered in a bubble,
And crying,
And can't tear myself free;
When really,

Bubbles are supposed to thought of as
Delightful, kind, free spirits who do not know
Where the breeze will take them next.
Hah.
When I get home, I wait for my mom to pop the
bubble,
A gesture in wait as the flowing river of my
day
Is released.
I'm free!
I take a soothing bath,
With Cherry Bubble Splash,
To help with the rest.
In my calm, relaxed state,
One lone bubble floats to my ear,
And it seemed as if it were whispering ever so
lightly:

"Being in a bubble is not always the best.
But as long as you have a special person to talk
to,
You shall be alright."

I will not forget that.
Whether it was a simple play of words
By my super busy mind,
Or a real-life bubble.

I now understand the beauty of being trapped
for a while,
Popped as thoughts, words, and images leak
out,
And then to be able to forget it with perhaps
just a bit of relaxation.

This it you people out there
Who feel caged in a bubble and can't break
free.
To those of us to cherish having someone
To talk to about troubling, stressful, and dumb
things.
        If only it were that easy. . .

April 14, 2011

Just Because

Just because I'm not speaking,
Does not mean I'm being silent.

Just because I'm on Honor Role,
Does not mean I get straight A's.

Just because I live in Wisconsin,
Does not mean I love on a farm.

Just because you apologize,
Does not mean you are forgiven.

Just because I'm a poet,
Does not mean I'm crazy about
Shakespeare.

Just because I speak my mind,
Does not mean I'm a bitch.

Just because you tell me what you want,
Does not mean I'll give it to you.

Just because I'm nice to my teachers,
Does not mean I'm a "teacher's pet."
Just because people get angry,
Does not mean that they don't care.

Just because we are in a fight,
Does not mean you can ignore my texts.

Just because I like to have fun,
Does not mean I'm crazy.

Just because I have a boyfriend,
Does not mean I get to see him everyday.

Just because I don't like basketball,
Does not mean I hate all sports.

Just because I have a job,
Does not mean I am swimming in cash.

Just because I love you,
Does not mean I will be fine if we ever
break up.

Just because I have to go,
Does not mean I want to stop talking.

Just because I have a different style,
Does not mean you can laugh at me.

Just because.

April 30, 2011

I Am

I am who I appear to be—
A nice, pretty girl who is almost happy.
I am who I appear to be.

A confident teenager who dares to wear
different things,
Such as combat boots and miniskirt.
I am who I appear to be.

A respectful student who says "good morning"
And "have a good afternoon" with a smile to
her teachers.
I am who I appear to be.

A kid who gets amused by silly little things,
Like skipping down the hall.
I am who I appear to be.

A person who loves choir and brings out notes
Other alto's fail to do.
I am who I appear to be.
A girl who cares about what she looks like,
And loves being complimented.

I am who I appear to be.

I do things that make me happy,
I could care less if what I do doesn't please
someone else.
I am who I appear to be.

I am very determined.
Even if I'm moments from throwing up,
I will continue moving forward during practice
and school.
I am who I appear to be.

I am NOT a quitter.
If my hip gets pulled and bruised in the middle
of a race,
I'll keep going.
I am who I appear to be.

I am also very sensitive,
I take everything too literally and get hurt.
This is I,
I am who I appear to be.

But, the things that don't appear to be,
Don't assume what they are.

Because most of the time,
Your assumptions are incorrect and hurtful
insinuations are made.
So, there is something you want to know that
doesn't appear to be,
Just simply ask.
Accusing and assuming hurts people very
badly.
thank you.
I am not who I appear to be.
April 26, 2012

Bethany

B elieves in ghosts
E very once in a while feels very insecure
T hinks boys are funny
H opes to be famous for writing one day
A lmost always smiles at school
N ot really into sports
Y es, she wrote this.

R ealizes that there are bigger things for her
A nyway she can help, she'd be glad to
Y appy when she talks with her best friends

D oesn't understand how people can be so mean
A nxious with a lot of things that happen
I ntuitive with certain topics in school
G estures crazily some days about certain things
L ets people hurt her feelings
E njoys watching movies and cuddling

October 12, 2010

Love

"Follow love and it will flee,
Flee love and it will follow thee."
- John Gay

Boy

I look at you,
You look at me.
You blush, then look away.
I smile to myself,
And think of the other day,
When you and me
Were meant to be.
You laughed, I smiled.
Everything seemed prefect while
She came.
She destroyed you and me.
Now I see that we are not meant to be.

April 14, 2010

You

You make me laugh all the time.
I cannot look at you and frown
While you are performing the face I love.
You impel me to forget simple things
When you kiss me, breathlessly.
You have me thinking that this is what heaven
Must be like during our hugs and hand-

holdings.
Please don't leave me,
I wouldn't be able to survive again.
Stay with me, baby.
I can't stop thinking about you,
No matter what I do.
Boy, I love you.
More than words can say.

May 15, 2010

You Are

My sunshine on a cloudy day.
My breath after I run.
My knight in shining armor.
My soft teddy bear.
The person I can turn to for some cheering up.
Someone I an talk to about nothing for hours.
A boy who knows when to be competitive
During a Wii game and
Cuddly during a movie.
A gentleman who gets the door for me,
An extrovert who says "hey, dude!"
To the people he doesn't know yet.

A friend I can confide in with everything.
Someone who makes me smile when he smiles.
A blondie who is an amazing kisser.
My laughter.
My boyfriend.
My love.
My husband, eventually.
My man.

April 17, 2011

Goodnight

It always starts with a few
"I love you's ."
Then we argue for a little bit about
About who loves who more.
Then we move on to some
"I miss you's," even though
you know I miss you more and
I know that you love me more.
Then there is a long pause.
You say "so…" in a melancholy tone,
That you wish I will have a
 Good night and that you
Will text me in the morning.

You remind me again that you love me. . . .
And that makes me have a great night's sleep.
Thanks, baby,
And goodnight!

August 18, 2010

Blue Eyes

Dear Blue Eyes,
Tell me what you see,
Is it he,
Who loves me so tenderly?
Tell me what you feel,
As he slowly starts to kneel
Onto his left leg,
His expression a silent, happy, beg.

Tell my why you worry,
There is no need for him to hurry.

He shall take his time,
And be ever-so-sublime.

Tell me why you are tired,
When you have just received what you desired.

Dear old blue eyes,
Tell me why this love
Is as significant as up above.

With everything sappy,
You are no less than happy.

Tell me why you hover
Off in the distance from your lover?
Always taking a gaze
That easily sees right through the haze.

Dear Blue Eyes,
Oh, for Heaven's sake
Don't forget to make those mistakes
That brought us here,
Everything is surrounding near.
March 3, 2012

LOVE

L ands in one's heart forever
O ver-rides all other thoughts
V ery beautiful and intriguing
E verything I've ever dreamed about
August 31, 2010

I Wanna

I wanna fall asleep texting you,
    like I always used to.

I wanna wake up remembering a dream,
    everything of "you and me."

I wanna see you wear that smile,
    even though it faded after a while.

I wanna let go,
    of everything I know.

I wanna throw my arms around you,
    letting my happiness easily show.

I wanna be that one girl,
    that lights up your world.

I wanna breathe that effortless breath,
    and know it will never again feel like
death.
I wanna be what I used to see.
        I wanna be the old "you and me."

July 28, 2012

Over You

After everything you've said to me,
After all the things you've done throughout
the months,
I've truly grasped the meaning of
"Will never be," so now I'm over you.
I have found someone great to take my place.
Don't worry about me anymore,
I for I won't worry about you, for once.
Though I will forget all the times
You said you'd call me,
I'll remember all the reasons people
Warned me to stay away from you.
They said you'd end up hurting me,
That "this" could never have happened,
That you were a bad choice.
I guess they were right.
I never wanted to believe them, but I had no
choice.
All that's left to say is that
I have turned the page
From dreaming of you
To BEING with him.
Toot-a-loo!

April 14, 2010

Broken Sigh

This reoccurring headache is the result of lack
of sleep.
Tossing and turning, flipping and flopping,
In search of some closure.
Some fake piece of fantasy that shatters my
reality,
Making a mere ludicrous figment that was
Strewn about haphazardly and lazily
Without a care or want or need.
It throbs like the heart in my chest,
Each beat painful.
There is no way to alleviate the ache,
Or even put it away for a moment.
Memories of red hearts and happy faces and
long, sweet kisses
Are burned at the stake.

I cannot forget what has happened.
I must remember the reason I bear the burden
Of being a permanent sad sap.
My laugh is horse, my smile cracked.
My eyes lack their glittery shine.
Instead of brightening a room by entering,
I cause a ruckus of stares, and whispers, and

thoughts to be spread.

The person I was before has vanished,
In a way.
Parts of her still linger here, in this being,
But only certain fragments remain intact.
She doesn't get ridiculously giddy over
anything,
Nor does she talk incessantly of the one
Who made her this way.

She stands straight and curt,
Perfectly appealing to any man by her stature.
Her expressions are now sullen and bleak,
Like she's constantly guarding her emotions
from
Dangerous thieves and murderers.

In her simple elegance,
Man wonders how she remains alone,
Without a fellow to link elbows with.
As they draw closer, they see, slowly,
The reason.

This girl is broken beyond repair
Of a hug or two and
Her humor is practically extinct.

When someone attractive comes nearby,
She gets awkward and silent.
She truly doesn't believe another man would
want her,
And yet,
She doesn't want to risk voiding this company.

She stays silent and occasionally mumbles a
response
To his conversation that is mostly with himself.
Her lack of confidence is greatly damaged,
Her happy morale is simply diminished.

This is a skeleton with bones
And flesh and feeling,
Of the girl who was here before.

This is me.

June 27, 2013

Meditation of a Break

On the eve of the final day of being sixteen,
She wonders about how she plundered so.

To make him switch,
And go to the dark side,
Possibly calling her a bitch.

She forces back the tears
She desperately hopes to hide.
The change occurred when no one knew,
When a magically drastic feat
So small began to grow.
Whole wide world she was now exposed to,
Lightened with a dark, dark hue.

The betrayal stands, and lingers in the mist
forever more.
The emotions sway to and fro along the edge of
the shore.
Horrific memories dance,
An awfully elucid,
Unfun,
Game of shame.

This Christmas Break, the worst gift she'd ever
received.
Insensitive texts make her feel different, a
product of being beseeched.
There she waddles, here she clocks.
A look turns into a stare, and she totally stops.

Not a horrible girl, but she may hurl.

Confused, dazed, and far from eternal bliss,
She feels absolutely broken among the great,
powerful abyss.

"I must not recollect what he said to me,"
she whispers under her breath,
"Being strong is key."

With fist of fury, eyes of stone, and a heart of
metal,

She decided he was nothing but a mere freckle,
Small, ugly, weak, and pointless.
A little smile and expressions of joy are
apparent upon her physique.

And with that, the girl went to sleep.
Without the opportunity to delete
What she had been through a few hours before,
As if scrawled out in front of her in cuneiform.

"Tomorrow is a new day," she thought.
"Although I may be flawed and distraught
from this onslaught,

I shall make something of me yet."

I shall make something of me yet.

December 22, 2013

What if?

What if one day, we broke up?
What if all of this was just a lie?
What if you knew you didn't love me anymore,
But decided not to tell me?
What if life as we both know it
Ended right there?
What if we never met someone
Better than the other?
What if we simply forgot everything
We have been through?
What if we continued our lives as if
We had not known one another?

What if?

April 20, 2011

About the Author

Bethany Ray Daigle was born in Duluth, Minnesota where she spent most of her youth. While living there, she met a girl two years older than her across Gilliat Street, Agne Kelley.

Agne was born in Lithuania and didn't speak English very well when she moved to the cute white house across from Bethany (who was 3) and her mother. With out being able to talk to one another right away, the two girls played Barbie's and dress-up all the time. They had adventures in the crick down the road and up the block. When Agne was diagnosed with liver cancer, Bethany didn't really understand what was going on. She had no idea that it would be what killed her best friend.
  "A Poem for Agne" is a commemorative piece, designated to express the thoughts and sadness still lingering 7 years after the fact of her passing.

Bethany is a happy person, and is amused and entertained with the smaller things in life, like rain and clouds. She has always been an intuitive writer, and hopes to take some writing classes when she goes off to college. In the fall semester of 2015, after she graduates high school that spring, she plans to attend University of Wisconsin Superior, to major in elementary education. From there, perhaps, she will move on in her career to be a high school English teacher.

She has always been 'weird,' in the sense that she does things out of the box. Bethany is not a typical teenage girl, for she wears suspenders and heels and paints mannequins for fun. Laughing and smiling just about all the time with everyone she meets, Bethany finds it very important to focus on the good things of life.

As a high school junior, Bethany was accepted into Cameron High School's National Honor Society organization, where she is excited about the community service and events she will participate in with her other classmates. Character will be built and perfected, while giving her a well-rounded look on resumes and college appilcations.

45885089R00037

Made in the USA
Lexington, KY
14 October 2015